3 9082 06584766 0

50.2/2018

D1261118

AUBURN HILLS PUBLIC LIBRARY
3400 E. Seyburn Drive
Auburn Hills, MI 48326

J46796126

50

17.50

TUNNELS

© 1994 Franklin Watts

First published in the United States in 1994 by
Franklin Watts
95 Madison Avenue
New York, NY 10016

Library of Congress Cataloging-in-Publication Data

Richardson, Joy.
    Tunnels / Joy Richardson.
        p. cm. — (Picture science)
    Includes index.
    ISBN 0-531-14290-6
    1. Tunnels — Juvenile literature. 2. Tunneling — Juvenile
literature. [1. Tunnels. 2. Tunneling.] I. Title. II. Series:
Richardson, Joy. Picture science.
TA807.R52 1994
    624.1'93—dc20   93-30057
                                                     CIP AC

10 9 8 7 6 5 4 3 2 1

Editor: Sarah Ridley
Designer: Janet Watson
Picture researcher: Sarah Moule
Artists: Robert and Rhoda Burns

Photographs: British Coal 10; Collections 9;
Frank Lane Picture Agency 7; Leslie Garland
Picture Library 14, 16; Robert Harding Picture
Library cover, 13, 23, 27; Planet Earth Picture
Library 19 (both); Q A Photos title page, 20, 24;
Derek Pratt/Waterways Picture Library 28.

All rights reserved

Printed in Malaysia

PICTURE SCIENCE

TUNNELS

AUBURN HILLS PUBLIC LIBRARY
3400 E. Seyburn Drive
Auburn Hills, MI 48326

Joy Richardson

FRANKLIN WATTS

New York • Chicago • London • Toronto • Sydney

Tunnel life

Lots of creatures dig tunnels
to make underground homes.

Rabbits make burrows, kicking out
the earth with their strong back legs.

Moles scratch away at the soil,
using their claws like shovels.
They make new tunnels each day,
searching for worms and insects.

Earthworms wriggle through the soil,
crisscrossing it with tunnels.
The soil passes through their bodies
and comes out as worm casts.

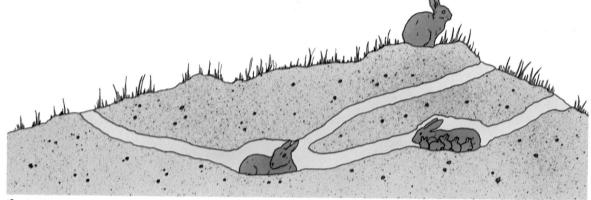

Natural tunnels

There are sometimes underground
tunnels and holes which no one has made.
Slowly, over millions of years,
the rock has been worn away by
dripping water and underground rivers.

Where there is a layer of soft rock
between layers of hard rock,
the soft rock may be worn away,
leaving a hard-rock ceiling.

Cave explorers study these
natural underground tunnels.

Mining

Thousands of years ago, mining began.
Some people used deer antlers to dig
tunnels through chalky rock.
They cut out flints which were
needed to make tools and weapons.

Today, coal, slate, gold, diamonds,
copper, iron, tin, and other metals
all come from mines.

When mining is finished, miles of
underground tunnels may be abandoned.

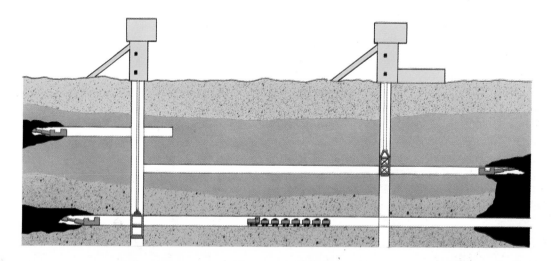

Taking a shortcut

It takes longer to travel around
or over the top of a mountain
than to go straight through it.

When canals became used often,
tunnels were cut through hills
to keep the canal water level.

Trains have difficulty climbing mountains,
so tunnels help to keep the
railroad tracks straight and flat.

Mont Blanc is a high mountain in Europe.
When a road tunnel was built through it,
the journey from France to Italy
was cut by 100 miles.

Water carriers

The longest tunnels in the
world do not carry traffic.
They carry water from place to place.

Networks of pipelines run to and
from reservoirs and dams,
water and sewage treatment plants,
power stations, factories, and houses.

These pipelines lie in shallow trenches.
Sections of pipe are fitted together
in the open trench and then covered over.

Deeper tunnels are cut through
the rock and then lined with concrete.

Underground trains

In big cities, the streets are very crowded, so many trains run underground.

The first underground train tunnels were built over a hundred years ago, in London.

A new invention, called a tunnel shield, moved slowly along the tunnels.
It supported the tunnel walls and protected the workers as they
drilled into the rock ahead.

Then the tunnel was lined with wide metal bands which were bolted together.

Now many cities have underground train tunnels beneath their streets.

Lying on the seabed

Tunnels cut through rock
on land or under the sea.
Tunnels can also lie on the seabed.
Some sunken tunnels carry trains or cars.

Huge lengths of steel tube
with sealed ends float
into place on the water.
Then they lower into channels
hollowed out in the seabed.

The sections are bolted together
and the joints are made watertight.
Workers cut through the seals
inside to open up the tunnel.

Crossing the water

The 31 mile tunnel between
Great Britain and France is the longest
underwater tunnel in the world.

Tunnel-boring machines cut through wet,
chalky rock far beneath the seabed.
They cut two tunnels for trains
and a service tunnel between them
for making repairs.

The tunnels were reinforced with concrete
and rings of metal to keep out water and
make the tunnel strong.

Cutting through rock

Tunnel-boring machines can cut away almost 300 feet of soft rock in a day. The front spins around at high speed. Sharp teeth eat into the rock face.

Soft, crumbly rock may need to be strengthened with cement before it is cut to stop it from falling down.

Very hard rock must be blasted. Machines called jumbos drill holes which are then filled with explosives. When the explosives are detonated, the rock comes tumbling down.

Tunnel-boring machine

Conveyor belt

Clearing the rubble

When the rock has broken down,
there is a lot of rubble on the ground.
This waste rock has to be cleared.
There may be thousands of tons.

In the past, the waste had to be shoveled
by hand into wagons and taken away.

Today, mechanical shovels
scoop up the rock.

Tunnel-boring machines are linked to
conveyor belts which carry the waste
and tip it into trucks.

All the cutting and clearing can
be done by machine.

Keeping the roof up

Almost all tunnels have rounded roofs. This helps stop the roof from being pushed in by the weight of rock or water above.

Soft rock collapses more easily than hard rock, so tunnels bored through soft rock need a strong lining.

Behind the tunnel-boring machine, huge curved plates of concrete or metal are lifted into place by machinery.

Any space between the walls and the lining is filled up with concrete to make the tunnel strong and watertight.

Tunnel facts

The longest tunnel in the world
is over 100 miles long.
It carries water to New York City.

The longest road tunnel is 10 miles
long, in Switzerland.

The longest railroad tunnel is in Japan.
It is 33 miles long.

The world's deepest tunnels are more
than 2 miles beneath the ground,
in gold mines in South Africa.

Index

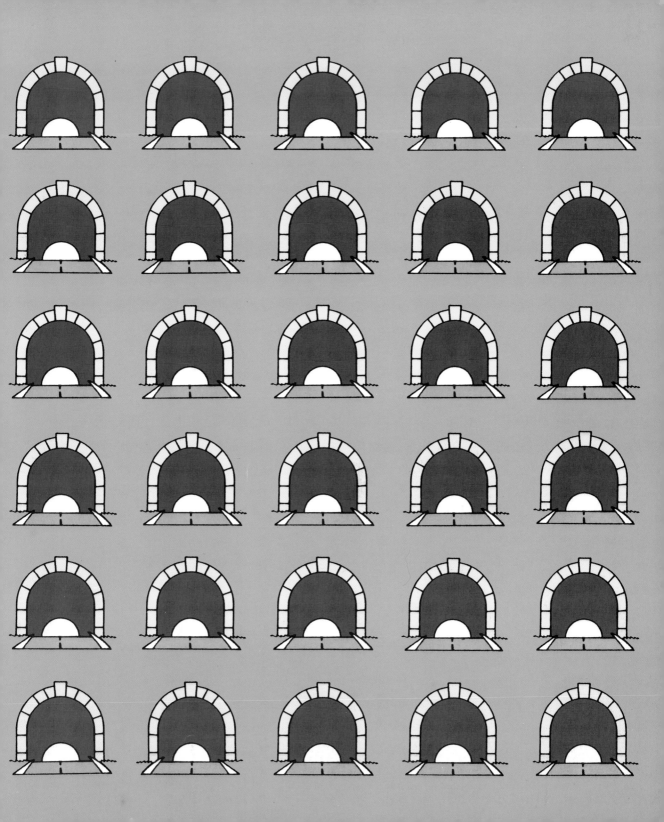